A Picture Book of
Thomas Jefferson

David A. Adler

illustrated by John & Alexandra Wallner

Holiday House / New York

To Michael, Eddie and Eitan
D.A.A.

For Bobby and John, with love
A.W. and J.W.

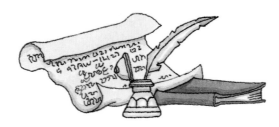

Library of Congress Cataloging-in-Publication Data
Adler, David A.
A picture book of Thomas Jefferson / written by David A. Adler :
illustrated by John and Alexandra Wallner.
p.   cm.
Summary: Traces the life and achievements of the architect,
bibliophile, president, and author of the Declaration of
Independence.
ISBN 0-8234-0791-8
1. Jefferson, Thomas, 1743-1826—Juvenile literature.
2. Presidents—United States—Biography—Juvenile literature.
[1. Jefferson, Thomas, 1743-1826.   2. Presidents.]   I. Wallner,
John C., ill.   II. Wallner, Alexandra, ill.   III. Title.
E332.79.A25   1990
973.4′6′092—dc20   89-20076   CIP
[B]   [92]
ISBN 0-8234-0791-8
ISBN 0-8234-0881-7 (pbk.)

Other books in David A. Adler's *Picture Book Biography* series

A Picture Book of George Washington

A Picture Book of Abraham Lincoln

A Picture Book of Martin Luther King, Jr.

A Picture Book of Thomas Jefferson

A Picture Book of Benjamin Franklin

A Picture Book of Helen Keller

A Picture Book of Eleanor Roosevelt

A Picture Book of Christopher Columbus

A Picture Book of John F. Kennedy

A Picture Book of Simón Bolívar

A Picture Book of Harriet Tubman

A Picture Book of Florence Nightingale

A Picture Book of Jesse Owens

A Picture Book of Anne Frank

A Picture Book of Frederick Douglass

A Picture Book of Sitting Bull

A Picture Book of Rosa Parks

A Picture Book of Robert E. Lee

A Picture Book of Sojourner Truth

A Picture Book of Jackie Robinson

A Picture Book of Paul Revere

A Picture Book of Patrick Henry

THOMAS JEFFERSON was born on April 13, 1743 in a four-room wooden house in Virginia. At that time Virginia was one of the thirteen American colonies that belonged to England.

Thomas was the third of ten children. He was tall and had red hair and freckles.

Young Thomas was curious and always eager to learn. He learned to hunt from his father. He learned how to plow, weave, and shoe a horse. Thomas made friends with Indians living nearby and learned from them, too.

When Thomas was fourteen, his father, Peter Jefferson, died. He left Thomas more than two thousand acres of land, his desk, his bookcase, and his library of some forty books.

Thomas loved to read. Those books were the beginning of his library. Many years later, he sold more than ten thousand of his books to the United States Congress. His books became an important part of the Library of Congress collection.

Peter Jefferson also left Thomas some slaves. The slaves were black people who were brought from Africa to America where they were sold. The slaves were used by their owners to plant and clear the fields, to cook and serve meals, and to take care of children.

Thomas Jefferson said he hated slavery. He said that everyone had a right to be free. When he was a member of the Virginia government he tried to pass laws ending the buying and selling of slaves. But still, throughout his life, he had slaves of his own.

When Thomas was sixteen, he went to the College of William and Mary in Williamsburg, Virginia. He worked hard and was a good student.

After he finished college, Thomas studied in the law office of his friend George Wythe. Then Thomas became a lawyer, too.

Thomas had ideas of his own about where he would live. In 1767 he designed and began to build a house for himself. He built it on a small mountain in Virginia, near where he was born. Thomas called the house Monticello which is Italian for "little mountain."

A few years later Thomas fell in love with Martha Wayles Skelton. She was a pretty, young widow. Thomas and Martha played music and sang together. They married on New Year's Day, 1772. They lived in Monticello.

Thomas and Martha had one son and five daughters. Only two of their daughters, Martha ("Patsy") and Mary ("Polly"), lived to be adults. Their other four children died when they were very young.

Thomas loved to invent useful things. He invented a better plow for farmers, a swivel chair, and a folding ladder. And he was open to new ideas. He was among the first Americans to take a vaccine to prevent small-pox.

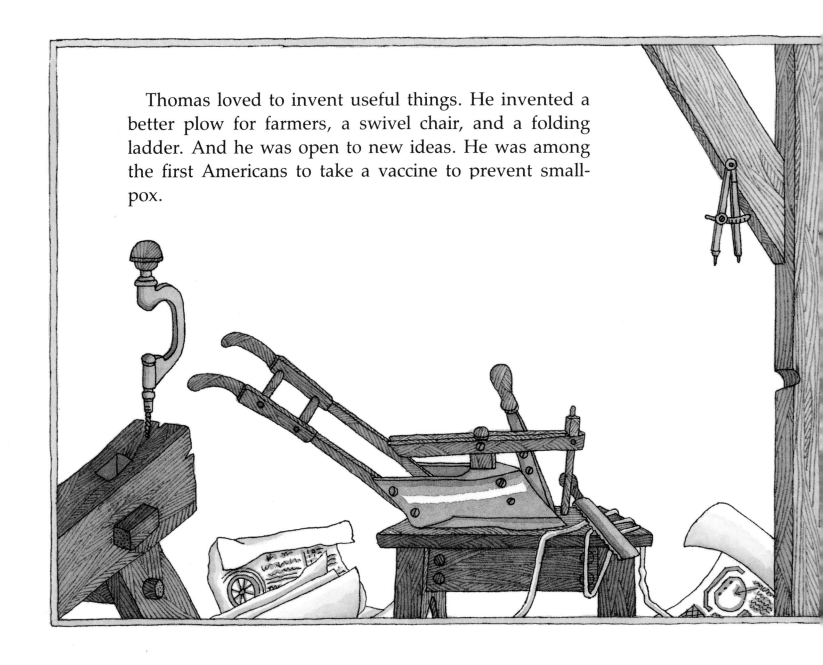

In 1768 Thomas was elected to the Virginia legislature, the House of Burgesses.

Members of the Virginia House of Burgesses and law-makers in other colonies were beginning to speak out against England. They felt that some of the English laws and the taxes in the colonies were unfair.

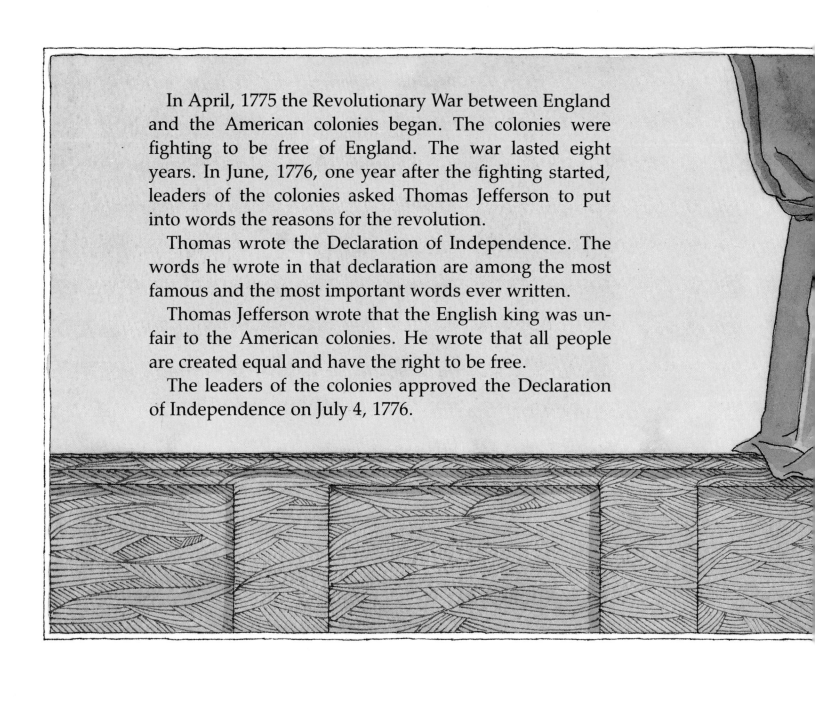

In April, 1775 the Revolutionary War between England and the American colonies began. The colonies were fighting to be free of England. The war lasted eight years. In June, 1776, one year after the fighting started, leaders of the colonies asked Thomas Jefferson to put into words the reasons for the revolution.

Thomas wrote the Declaration of Independence. The words he wrote in that declaration are among the most famous and the most important words ever written.

Thomas Jefferson wrote that the English king was unfair to the American colonies. He wrote that all people are created equal and have the right to be free.

The leaders of the colonies approved the Declaration of Independence on July 4, 1776.

During the war, Thomas Jefferson was elected governor of Virginia for two terms. Then he was elected to the Continental Congress. While in the Congress, he helped to pass the Treaty of Paris of 1783, which ended the Revolutionary War.

After the war, Thomas was sent to France as a representative of the new United States. While Thomas Jefferson was there, the new American government was set up. A constitution was written. And George Washington was elected the first president of the United States.

George Washington asked Thomas Jefferson to be his secretary of state. He would represent the United States in its dealings with other nations.

In 1796 John Adams was elected the second president of the United States. Thomas Jefferson was elected his vice president.

Four years later, in 1800, Thomas Jefferson was elected the third president of the United States. In 1804 he was reelected for a second term. He was a very popular president.

Thomas didn't want people to make a fuss over him. He didn't want the country to celebrate his birthday, so he didn't tell anyone when it was. And he didn't wear fancy clothes like many people thought he should.

As president, Thomas Jefferson lowered taxes. He sent American soldiers to fight a group of pirates in northern Africa. During his term, the land between the Mississippi River and the Rocky Mountains became part of the United States. The land, purchased from France, was called the Louisiana Purchase.

After his second term as president, Thomas Jefferson returned to Monticello.

During his later years, Thomas Jefferson helped to start the University of Virginia.

Many people came to visit him at Monticello. And many people wrote to him. Thomas Jefferson offered his visitors a meal and a place to sleep.

On July 4, 1826, Thomas Jefferson died exactly fifty years after the Declaration of Independence had been approved.

Thomas Jefferson was one of our country's great leaders. He believed that all people had a right to be free. He believed that people should govern themselves. That is why he has been called the Father of Our Democracy.

IMPORTANT DATES

1743	Born on April 13 in Virginia.
1769–1775	Served in the Virginia House of Burgesses.
1772	Married Martha Wayles Skelton on January 1.
1776	Wrote the Declaration of Independence.
1779–1781	Governor of Virginia.
1782	Martha Jefferson, his wife, died.
1785–1789	Minister to France.
1790–1793	Secretary of State in President Washington's cabinet.
1797–1801	Vice President of the United States.
1801–1809	President of the United States.
1826	Died on July 4 in his home, Monticello.

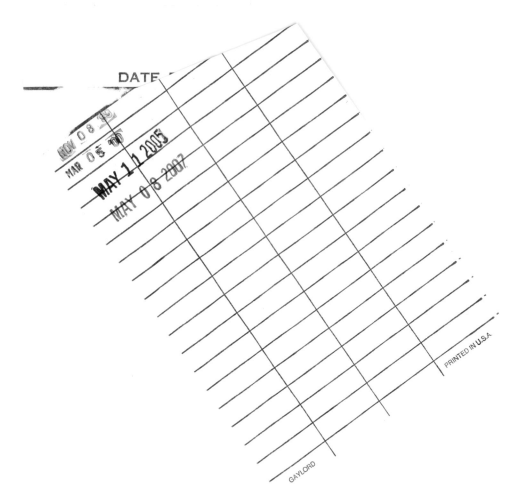

DATE

NOV 0 8

MAR 0 8

MAY 1 1 2005

MAY 0 8 2007

PRINTED IN U.S.A.

GAYLORD